I enjoyed lunches and dinners with myself.

I took walks on the park with myself.

I traveled by myself.

I told myself daily how much I loved myself.

I had conversations with myself. Now that might sound a little crazy to you, but my dad once told me that sometimes when I needed stimulating/intelligent conversation, I need to speak to and answer myself.

I took bubble baths by myself.

I nurtured myself.

The same energy I had put into loving someone else I put into loving myself.

As I loved myself, I made note of the things and places I enjoyed most. I made note of what made me happy, sad, disappointed, etc.

I journaled every day and as a result I was able to put together a realistic list of the way I wanted my future partner to love and cherish me.

As I loved me, I took note of the characteristics I wanted my future partner to possess and I also compiled a list of boundaries as well as a list of things that were not negotiable for me.

At the end of my first year of loving me and not relying on someone else to validate and love me, I felt whole for the first time in a pretty long time.

During this period of time, I enjoyed the company of my inner circle friends as well.

Apart from working together on common goals, we also socialized together. I found joy in these rich friends and learned that love does not necessarily have to be romantic. It could come in many forms.

I also enjoyed our family gatherings more. I think this was because I was not so distracted by my partner or by some situation caused by him that had me in emotional turmoil.

I realized that love was not something I needed to search for; it was something I already had.

As I focused on me which included my self-development and enjoying new hobbies, I found I had a greater sense of peace.

I learned to understand and more importantly love me.

While focusing on building me and on serving in my community, one day, just like magic, he appeared.

He stood outside my gate as my friends and I were getting ready to leave on my annual birthday adventure.

What amazed me is that I did not search him out; he found me.

I won't for a single moment lead you to believe that it was all fairy tales and roses from there because it was not but what I did find was that I was ready and prepared to handle the responsibility of a lasting love relationship.

I was no longer fully dependent on someone else to love and fulfill me. I was able to do that for myself and whatever he did only added to my joy.

I had not found my knight in shining amour nor had a prince come to rescue a distraught maiden. I found myself involved in a relationship with a man who truly loved and respected me.

In my Bible, the word of God taught me that "He who finds a wife finds a good thing." He found me.

Today, I believe in love not in the crazy overly romantic love that we have been taught to seek but a realistic love where there is mutual respect, support and caring.

I believe in a perfect love with an imperfect person.

I still smile when I think about the ways he touches my heart and while he is not a romantic by any stretch of the word, he is a gentlemen, he is thoughtful, he is affectionate, he is appreciative, he speaks into me, he encourages me, he is walking alongside mem he is super supportive and we are creating the future we both want with each other.

I had given up on love; thrown in the towel and decided that love was for the birds but when I took the time to completely love and accept me my romantic love appeared.

I was preparing myself for a king the entire time and did not know it.

I was healing the broken parts of me so that I could offer myself to him as healthy, whole and healed person.

We can enjoy imperfect relationships when we love ourselves and accept ourselves as imperfect.

We set ourselves up for disappointment by expecting happily ever after without bumps and challenges.

The beauty of the imperfect love is navigating those challenges and growing together in partnership.

Now I am so happy and believe that true love, real love is possible.

I wake up to it every single day as a wife who is accepting and supportive of her imperfect husband.

**Tips to love yourself:**

1. **Enjoy your own company.**

2. **Date yourself.**

3. **Create healthy boundaries.**

4. **Stop sabotaging yourself by removing the negative messages you tell yourself and replace them with more positive message.**

5. **Create or find affirmations and speak them over your life daily.**

6. **Discover and enjoy your strengths.**

**7. Spend time with positive people.**

**8. Stimulate yourself by staying on a continuous growth journey.**

**9. Relax and rejuvenate.**

**After reading today's entry, I realize:**




**Today I want to focus and work on:**




**Today's affirmation:**
I love myself.

I am amazing, talented, and worthy.

I love everything about me even the parts of me that need improvement.

I love me.

I love the people around me.

I understand they are not perfect, and I love them as imperfect beings.

I will give love to those I encounter every day.

I deserve love.

I will receive love every day.

My relationships will be based on love.

I will attract love into my life by being the best version of me I can possibly be.

I will not seek out romantic love; I will attract it.

Loving me is the first steps towards a healthy relationship.

Loving me teaches others how to love me.

I am worthy of a healthy love.

I deserve to be loved and cherished.

I am whole. I am fierce. I am brilliant. I am beautiful. I am amazing. I am an overcomer. I am a Queen.

**Today's reflections:**

**When it comes to loving yourself, what are you most resistant to?**

**Of the items you were most resistant to, which can you work on?**

## Day 18 - Failure

We all dread the F word, but failure is part of life.

To the perfectionist failure is like a death sentence.

I have rebounded from failure many times. In the early years, failure was fatal to me. In my later years, failure became the pathway to success.

We beat ourselves up, over-think the situation and torture ourselves for not taking different actions.

When we fail, we take it to heart and begin to have symptoms of a physical illness. Yes, it is that serious!

You have failed a time or two in your life I'm sure! Failure is not final. How did you use failure to make a strong come back?

Now I have failed many times. Failing repeatedly did not make dealing with failure any easier. Each time I failed, I was harder on myself than the last time.

Let me tell you about some of my experiences with failure.

I failed my first driving test. Can you imagine that? I had followed the instructions; completed the three-point turn, used the car signals, answered the questions correctly but I knocked one of those dreadful orange cones which was an automatic fail. I was devastated and I was so embarrassed!!!

I failed at my first marriage. Yes, I know it was not totally my fault but that does not make it any better. I promised to honor, love and respect until death do us part and I am still alive. Why was I not I a better wife? Why wasn't I able to make the difference in his life? Not only had I failed at marriage, but also failed at other romantic relationships.

I failed at my first business. I opened a small kindergarten and nursery. I prepared the space creatively. I had purchased the stimulating activities and created a play area to die for. I advertised and walked the neighborhood handing out flyers and talking to the residents. On the day that the kindergarten and nursery opened two children registered. It was a struggle to continue and I tried for a few months to build the business, advertising more and trying to get more students registered. I eventually ended up having to close due to lack of business. I failed to make this business successful.

I have failed numerous times over the course of my life, but I have learned to look at failures different.

Failing means I took action; I tried something, and it didn't work out, but I gave it my best effort.

For each time I failed in the past or when I fail today, I look at the experience as a learning one. What went wrong? What went well? What could be different next time? Instead of solely licking my wounds I now take the time to use the lessons to fail forward.

I am encouraged to continue chasing my dreams because I realize that many of the successful people in the world failed before becoming successful.

People like Bill Gates, Steve Jobs, Milton Hersey and even Michael Jordan were failures.

I am most encouraged by the failure of Walt Disney.

Walt Disney was fired from the newspaper company he worked at and told he was just not creative. Imagine that. He formed his very first animation company but was forced to close it. He did not give up. Despite his failures, he pressed on. Today Disney World is a playground that children and adults flock to. It is a place filled with imagination and creativity.

We should take Denis Waitley's reminder about failure to heart. "*Failure should be our teacher, not our undertaker. Failure is delay, not defeat. It is a temporary detour, not a dead end. Failure is something we can avoid only by saying nothing, doing nothing and being nothing.*"

**Tips to overcome failure:**

1. **Acknowledge your feelings.**

2. **Refine failure as something more positive.**

3. **Focus on the lesson the experience provides.**

4. **Build your resiliency muscles by getting back in the game.**

5. **Create action plans to incorporate the lessons into a future attempt.**
6. **Congratulate yourself for acting.**
7. **Move forward.**

**After reading today's entry, I realize:**

**Today I want to focus and work on:**

**Today's affirmation:**

I am fearless.

I will not allow the fear of failure to hold me back from acting.

I understand that failure is a part of life.

I will learn valuable lessons when I fail.

Failure will make me stronger.

I will overcome challenges while staying positive.

I am strong and resilient.

Despite failure I will be successful.

I will act despite my fear.

I am fierce. I am brilliant. I am beautiful. I am amazing. I am an overcomer. I am a Queen.

**Today's reflections:**


**When being rebounding from failure, what are you most resistant to?**




**Of the items you were most resistant to, which can you work on?**

## Day 19 - Beliefs

How are our beliefs formed?

According to my research, *"beliefs can come from two sources: our own experiences and reflections, or as blind acceptance of what other people tell us."*

My beliefs about myself during my early age were formed by my experiences.

After Mother, my primary nurturer died, I was left to deal with the sorrow and emptiness with little to no support.

As a result of not being validated as a child and not taught skills that reinforced a healthy self-esteem, I believed I was unworthy of love.

My experiences with men during my teenage years taught me to believe that men were all after my "precious stuff". Men just wanted to get with me to satisfy their sexual urges. It also taught me that men could not be trusted.

Those experiences also helped me to believe that men were not faithful. There were men who solicited me when they were already in committed relationships.

My marriage experience helped me to believe that I was worthy of punishment and when I angered my ex-husband it was acceptable for him to beat me.

I believed I deserved to be beaten because had I been a better wife, he would not have lashed out at me.

Due to my low esteem and lack of self-value, I did not believe in my talents or skills.

Even when people referred to my strengths or paid me compliments, I shook them off and found reasons to contradict them.

I was told I would not amount to anything and that I would never make it in life. Those words beat me down and helped me to believe that I was unworthy of embracing my potential and living to my fullest potential.

I found myself "dumbing" down so others would not be uncomfortable. I hid my radiance and my brilliance because who was I to shine?

I was uncomfortable with conflict because I valued people more than I valued myself.

My beliefs were the reason I lived a substandard life.

I let go of my dreams and goals when Mother died.

I did not believe it was possible for me to live them out but thank goodness for the mentorship I received which revived my dreams.

My mentor was instrumental in shifting my mindset and reframing my past. As I grew under his mentorship, I started to believe in me.

We often believe that reaching our for help is a sign of weakness when in fact it is a characteristic of the strong.

We get stuck and are embarrassed to seek help. Our pride keeps us stuck!

Our beliefs can change! We can replace the negative beliefs with more positive ones. We will need to heal from our experiences and to create new experiences to replace those old ones to give us something to latch onto.

You have access to people, tools, resources that can help you move past self-limiting beliefs. You can choose to seek help and support.

It is critical to inspect your beliefs. What you believe is possible is and what you believe is impossible will be.

As you think about your life, what have you been believing? How have your beliefs been holding you back?

I had to go to the root of my self-limiting beliefs and prove to myself that they were false.

I had to prove that they were lies and I had to replace the lies with the truth.

I could only replace them with the truth once I knew what my truth was.

The journey to self-discovery is a necessary one to embark upon. It is a continuous and ongoing journey.

Taking the time to find out why you do what you do, or why you do not do what you want to do, is necessary for your success.

I had to figure out what was shaping my thoughts and then shift through the thoughts until I found the truth.

I now believe in myself, in my dreams, goals, talents and skills.

I know that anything I put my mind to I can achieve.

I no longer "dumb" myself down, ignore my passion, or hide my brilliance.

I fully embrace all that is me because I believe in me.

**Tips to build change your beliefs:**

1. **Identify your self-limiting beliefs by writing them down on paper.**

2. **Then inspect them.**
    a. **Are they true?**
        i. **If not write the truth underneath the statement**

    b. **If they, do you want to accept or change them?**

3. **Research and find out where your beliefs stem from. Are they really yours?**
  .
4. **Visualize your ideal future. See the person you want to be.**

**5. Create daily affirmations to address and help to change your beliefs about yourself.**

**After reading today's entry, I realize:**

**Today I want to focus and work on:**

**Today's affirmation:**

My current situation is attached to what I believe.

I will begin the process of changing my self-limiting beliefs with limitless beliefs.

My beliefs drive my behavior.

I know that what I believe I am is what I will become.

I will no longer allow my beliefs to subconsciously control me.

I will inspect them, challenge them, and heal any parts of me that cause me to doubt me.

I know that I am the master of me so I will control negative thoughts and replace any negative self-beliefs with positivity.

I believe in my abilities and I believe in me.

I am fierce. I am brilliant. I am beautiful. I am amazing. I am an overcomer. I am a Queen.

**Today's reflections:**

**What are you most resistant to when thinking about changing your beliefs?**

*Of the items you were most resistant to, which can you work on?*

## Day 20 - Seeing Your Value

One of my closest friends always told me that I did not see myself clearly.

She still is one of my greatest supporters and pushes me to chase my dreams even when they sound outrageous.

She has always been a great support and has always believed in me.

She would scold me when I allowed people to take advantage of my talents.

I had not established proper boundaries as yet and she would encourage me to put some boundaries in place so I that I would not be taken advantage of.

Amazingly, each time we had this discussion, I tried to understand what she was taking about.

What exactly would people try to take advantage of?

How were they robbing me?

How was I being used?

What was so great about my skills? They were effortless to me so what was she talking about?

When a former boss told me that I was influential I wondered what she was talking about. I was an ordinary person like anyone else. There was nothing special about me.

I did not understand at that point that my desire to be accepted was the driving force behind me seeking the approval of others by giving, giving, giving or by doing, doing, doing.

When we see our value and begin to appreciate what we bring to the table it changes the game.

After years of fighting self-doubt and having an extremely low self-esteem, I was conditioned to believe that I was unworthy and therefore anything I had to offer was also worthless.

You see self-esteem is at the base of how we see ourselves and quite frankly I did not see much in me.

We overlook the good qualities we possess and focus on our weakness. It is something we have been trained to do.

On jobs they want us to develop our weaknesses even when those are unnecessary to complete our tasks. Acknowledging and functioning in our strengths is a much better strategy!

I can vividly remember a relationship I had a few years ago. It is a significant memory because whenever I think about how much I did not appreciate my value; I remember how my then partner was no longer emotionally invested in the relationship but was reluctant to let me go.

My ex found value in the relationship because of the way he benefited even without the emotional investment.

This was not a mutually beneficial relationship because he got the benefit of someone willing to join him on his journey towards achieving his goals without having to reciprocate.

As a matter of fact, my need to belong kept me in the relationship even though I knew I was not happy.

Whenever we discussed terminating the relationship, my ex would say that he did not want to because I was such a good person. His family loved me. Whenever he found himself in a difficult situation, he could count on me to help pull him out of it. If he was working a project, he had a helpmate to work along with him. His success was my priority. I put more energy into him, his family, and his success than I put into mine.

As frustrated as I was in the relationship, his happiness meant more to me than mine.

Have you had any of these experiences?

As I worked with my mentor and looked back on these types of experiences where I did not appreciate myself and what value I added, I learned several lessons.

The most important lesson I took away from those reflection exercises, was that I needed to improve my self-esteem and learn to see myself clearly.

Who was I?

Who did I want to be known as?

What were my strengths?

How did I add value to others in the past?

What were the skills and talents that the people around me benefit most from?

What did I need to do to affirm myself?

Why was I uncomfortable with my physical beauty? Should I embrace it?

The bottom line is......... I needed to see my value and to do so I needed to wade through the mud puddle of my stored emotions.

Once I had done so I realized that I really loved the person I had unearthed and wanted to be a much better and improved version of her.

Know that poor self-worth and poor self-value keep us trapped in places we should not be and restrict us from fully living life.

Discover who you are. Begin to appreciate you.

Improve your self-esteem by completing your daily affirmations, by discovering new talents and skills, create goals you want to achieve, serve others, get a mentor, keep learning and growing, surround yourself with good people and focus on loving the person you are.

***Tips to value yourself:***

1. ***Do not compare yourself with others.***

2. ***Identify your strengths and talents. Accept and enjoy your passions.***

3. ***Celebrate your uniqueness.***

**4. Stop settling while thinking you do not deserve better.**

**5. Do not make temporary situations permanent.**

**6. Give yourself room to grow.**

**7. Establish healthy boundaries.**

**8. See the value you bring. Ask others if you are unsure.**

**After reading today's entry, I realize:**




**Today I want to focus and work on:**

***Today's affirmation:***

I love and value me.

I approve of myself and do not need the approval of others to validate me.

I do not need to prove my worthiness to others, nor do I need to work to be accepted.

I appreciate my strengths.

I will take conscious note of when I make decisions because I want affirmation and validation.

I am valuable to the people around me, the organization I work at and the affiliations I am associated with.

I know that I am unique and my difference from others is what makes me unique.

I will value those differences.

I deserve all the good I can possibly get.

I attract goodness because I am good to others.

God valued me enough to allow my presence to fill the earth.

I will honor who I am.

I am fierce. I am brilliant. I am beautiful. I am amazing. I am an overcomer. I am a Queen.

**What are you most resistant to when it comes to seeing your value?**

**Of the items you were most resistant to, which can you work on?**

# Day 21 - Intentional Action

Today I live a fulfilled life. This is due mostly in part to the intentional actions I take daily. I feel excited about life! I am grateful. I feel a sense of purpose and of peace.

After figuring out and accepting my life's purpose, I began to take the steps required to full that purpose.

My vision for my life is to be a credible, solutions oriented and impactful leader. I want to be recognized as an expert in my field in the country I live in and the world. I commit to continued personal growth and development so that I can add value to my team and be the kind of leader my team is proud and happy to be associated with.

My life's purpose is to impact lives, particularly young lives and help them to overcome their traumatic experiences to live their life's purpose and to live the best life they possible can.

After I identified my purpose, everything that I did tied back into it. I had to be deliberate in achieving my goals and ensuring that my goals tied back into my overall vision for my life.

We live a more fulfilled life when we know who we are, when we define what success means to us and when we live life on our terms, authentically and purposely.

Are you living your best life today?

To live my best life, anything that distracted or tried to pull me away from my purposed had to be eliminated.

I knew that I would face challenges along my life's journey and so I created a plan to follow when distractions or setbacks occurred.

I preferred not to handle those situations when I was emotional.

By having a plan to revert to, I made sure I could make sound decisions and be intentional about my actions.

I worked improve my brand. Joining organizations that focused on self-development and organizations that served the less fortunate, helped me to stay on a continuous growth journey.

I created vision boards for reminders about what I was ultimately trying to achieve.

I filled a white board with my goals broken down into smaller steps and as I accomplished each one, I crossed it off and celebrated myself.

Looking at the board with goals crossed off fueled my passion.

I also changed my circle. I found the company of women and men who were focused on making a difference in the world and together we worked on assisting each other achieve our goals.

I aligned myself with mentors and coaches who all held me accountable for accomplishing my goals. They along with my accountability partner reminded me of what I was working toward and our meetings forced me to stay focused. I did not want to waste anyone's time, nor did I want to waste the money I had invested in my coaches.

We must take action to recreate ourselves, to learn to make better choices, to identify our limiting self-beliefs and to heal any trauma from past broken or traumatic experiences.

This is a key step in our success!

You are the solution you are looking for. No one else can change your situation or your life. Living your happiest and best life depends on what you do with your now.

My intentional actions have helped me to jump some hurdles, accomplish my goals and impact my world.

As a result of the work I did to heal myself and to then reinvent myself I am living a purpose driven life.

Working on myself was the first step. We attract energies into our lives based on the energy we send out into the world. Becoming a better person helped me to attract and to develop a better life.

I am living out loud and being intentional about my steps because I want to truly live my best life while living my life's purpose.

**Tips on how to be intentional:**

    ***1. Create your life's vision.***

    ***2. Identify what your picture goals are.***

    ***3. Create goals that tie into that vision.***

    ***4. Create action steps to make your goals reality.***

    ***5. Create a daily schedule.***

6. *Prioritize highest to lowest importance items.*

7. *Put them in your calendar and refer to your calendar daily.*

8. *Identify time wasters and avoid them.*

9. *Identify distractions and manage them.*

10. *Every day, take actions that align with your vision and that will help you to achieve your goals.*

11. *Reflect on your actions every week to ensure they align with your big picture goals.*

12. *Tweak as necessary.*

*After reading today's entry, I realize:*

**Today I want to focus and work on:**




**Today's affirmation:**

I will be intentional about living my life's purpose.

I am intentional about embracing my passions.

I will take the steps required to achieve my dreams and goals.

I will stop doing the things that will derail my efforts.

I will be intentional about using my strengths and I will be intentional about my growth.

I will find opportunities to continue to develop.

I will use my time wisely.

I understand that my gifts are not for me but to benefit others so I will be intentional about how I use my skills and talents.

I will treat others well.

I will take care of my mind, body, and spirit.

I will honor the divine in me.

I am fierce. I am brilliant. I am beautiful. I am amazing. I am an overcomer. I am a Queen.

**Today's reflections:**

**When being self-aware, what were you most resistant to?**

**Of the items you were most resistant to, which can you work on?**

# Coming Out of the Haze - A New Day Has Come

As I reflect on the journey, I took to the new improved version of me, I acknowledge that it took more than twenty-one days.

The reality is the journey is never ending.

The key is to start and that is what this book was designed to do. Jump-start the journey towards a better life.

A great life: an abundant and happy life is ahead. We can claim this life when we do the "work" necessary to live it.

We have the power and too often we let our power remain dormant.

The power is there for us to use it. Reach deep inside of you and reclaim your power Sister! It is there, waiting on you to take action!

Understand that there may be hazy days, but you have the tools to help clear the haze away and make choices to improve your tomorrows.

Do not give in when you make mistakes or repeat patterns.

The healing process will not be an overnight one. It is a journey.

It is a one step, one day at a time situation. Embrace the journey to a better you.

On my journey, there were issues I wanted to avoid. There were experiences I did not want to remember and lessons I did not want to learn.

There was no choice though. If I wanted to move past my limitations and overcome my challenges, I had to face myself. I had to understand what motivated me to continue making poor choices and decisions so that I could begin to make better ones.

Know that you can always make another choice. You do not have to be stuck.

Get to know who you are, what you are about, what you want out of life and what you want your legacy to be then chase after it relentlessly and passionately.

Align yourself with good people. Find mentors who are willing to pour into you and to help you shift through the muddiness of your best to create a much better future. Find a coach to help you introspect and project.

Create an inner circle of friends who you can push to achieve their goals and who will help you to stay focused on yours.

Create your vision boards. Write your goals out. Keep them visible.

Do not be afraid of what is to come. Know that whatever lies ahead of you can be greater than what you have laid behind you.

Fall in love with yourself. Learn to love the parts of you that you find unlovable. Change the parts of you that you find necessary to change. Embrace your uniqueness. Embrace your brilliance.

Embrace your experiences. They have made you the strong person you are today. Yes YOU! You are stronger than you realize. You are still alive and there is a reason for that. Find that reason and hold on to it. Be obedient to the call on your life. God has a purpose for you to fulfill. Fulfill it.

Always be true to yourself and see the truth in every situation. Be honest with you and at the same time be gentle with yourself.

You have the power!

I am overwhelming grateful for the opportunity to share my experiences with you.

It is another intentional step in my journey to impact women positively.

We create community, when we help others along the journey, when we share our lessons and our experiences.

We all need to know that we are not alone.

We are inspired when we see other sisters being resilient and turning broken experiences into success stories.

As you journey on, know that you can always come back to the book to refresh yourself on any lesson as often as you need it.

Be open to accepting what you receive from it and to putting into practice the steps necessary for you to improve your life, overcome your limitations and challenges and to live your best life.

Remember, I am your sister in love, here to help you along with journey and I am rooting for you!

## Other Valuable Resources

## *The Evolving Woman Video Affirmation Guide*

*In just twenty-one-days, you will feel more powerful after affirming and validating yourself.*

*This video series has helped hundreds of women, release the need for external sources to valid them and have learnt to affirm their worth and value.*

https://duquesadean.com/index.php/tv/subscribe-to-affirmations-21-day-journey

# Credits:

*Cover Design by Winston Dean*

www.ingramcontent.com/pod-product-compliance
Lightning Source LLC
Chambersburg PA
CBHW070851050426
42453CB00012B/2131